SLA | GUIDELINES

Planning and Designing
a Secondary School
Library Resource
Centre

Leonore Charlton

Series Editor: Geoff Dubber

School Library Association

The School Library Association is an independent organisation and registered charity which was founded in 1937 to promote the development of libraries in schools. Today the SLA exists to support and encourage all those working in school libraries, raising awareness and promoting good practice through an effective training and publications programme. Membership of the Association brings many benefits including an advisory/information service for national and international enquiries, an excellent quarterly reviewing journal, and reduced rates for all publications and training courses. For full details, contact the SLA office in Swindon (address and telephone number below).

Acknowledgements

The author would like to thank Stephen Gower of Demco Interiors for the layouts on pages 24 and 25, and Geoff Dubber for his useful comments on them. She would also like to thank Kathy Lemaire and Dianne Southcombe for their helpful comments on the revised manuscript.

Published by the School Library Association
Unit 2, Lotmead Business Village
Lotmead Farm, Wanborough
Swindon SN4 0UY
Tel: 01793 791787
Fax: 01793 791786
e-mail: publications@SLA.org.uk

Designed by Harriet Eagle
Printed by Will Print, Oxford

Contents

Introduction

The aim of this publication is to provide librarians, library managers and those new to the profession with ideas and guidelines for the planning and design of a school library resource centre (LRC). Experienced librarians in school library services have for some time been closely involved – in partnership with schools, LEA property departments and architects – with the design and layout of new and refurbished LRCs. These thoughts attempt to encapsulate that experience.

In order to plan and design an appropriate and effective LRC it is essential that its overall school role, staffing structures, management and planned developments for learning are contemplated and considered. Decisions on these factors will greatly influence the principal ideas for the design. The use of the library resource centre needs to be planned within a whole-school learning skills policy and this should develop via the overall delivery of the curriculum by each department. It may also be useful to consider the school's wider community role at this stage.

The learning resources

The concept of a library resource centre is changing rapidly – in the light of the growing importance of ICT, recent literacy initiatives and an awareness of the importance of inclusion. There is an increasing focus on the development of learning and literacy skills, with the emphasis less on a physical collection of books and materials, and more on reader development and the expertise required to find and use information and develop skills in areas of information handling.

A school will acknowledge the need for an LRC if it understands and accepts an ethos of whole-school and cross-curricular use of information. Such a library will encompass a greater range of learning resources, enabling improved and more comprehensive services to be available. The nature and range of these resources and services must be considered carefully at the planning and design stage.

Information is presented in many formats and thought must be given to the balance between the different types of resources that students and teaching staff will need, not only now but in the future. The installation of ICT workstations and equipment will need to have a high priority. Consideration must also be given to storage conditions and the availability of equipment for the use of various resources. Careful planning of the layout of the centre and the arrangement of the collections will make it easier for teachers and students to make maximum use of all types of stock and information.

Learning resources can be defined as any type of material which contributes positively to the learning process. The following resources are relevant in a secondary school LRC and all require specialist or particular methods of storage to be visible and easily accessible:

- books and pamphlets, in hardback and paperback format, suitable for children and adults and presenting factual and fictional information

- periodicals and newspapers providing current information in an easily acceptable format

- other paper-based resources: wall charts, maps, results of field studies courses, study folders, and portfolios of numerous items including ephemera, newspaper cuttings and postcards

- computer software: wordprocessing, spreadsheets and graphics applications; CD-ROM discs to be used with stand-alone machines or over a network for access to large databases using sophisticated searching techniques

- Internet, intranet and video conferencing facilities

- film/visual material – videos, DVDs, photographs (including copies and possibly originals of old photographs), micro-film (for example, census returns and newspapers), overhead projector transparencies from commercial sources, Power point presentations and in-house productions and videos

- audio material: cassette tapes and CDs of sounds, stories, music and documentary material

- artefacts, including models, specimens, and kits

- multimedia packs

- collections of materials in various formats dealing with specific topics.

Which resources?

Decisions on which resources are to be held in the centre will be based upon:

- knowledge of the curriculum
- the need to augment literacy skills and reading development
- the need to develop information handling skills
- the need to foster students' personal interests
- the location and potential of the library.

The balance between the central learning collection and the departmental collections will need careful thought. Reorganising or planning a new resource centre are unique opportunities to involve subject specialists in looking critically at the resources used and stored across the school. Storage in the LRC encourages cross-curricular use and the exploitation of materials, and introduces economies of scale. This may be an appropriate time to consider the incorporation of departmental resources into the collection or, at the very least, to provide access to departmental collections through electronic cataloguing.

Now is also the time to deal with inappropriate stock and out-of-date items. Discard them! Stock development should be planned to balance all collections held within the school. See SLA Guideline *Shelf Life, Shelf Matters* for ideas of ways to carry out this task (details on page 22).

The design of the library resource centre must take into account its central role. Staff from across the school – senior managers, subject specialists, library staff, technicians – and also students should be involved in identifying the scope and needs of the centre. It will be useful to consider and plan the following aspects:

Plenty of space

- flexible and adequate space to accommodate groups, classes and individuals – particularly if the school has a large sixth form group who regularly use the LRC for private study
- room for sufficient computers and appropriate work space for each PC (remembering this is not an ICT suite)
- ventilation – it is vital to ensure that there is sufficient ventilation for the users' comfort, and to consider the heat generated by computers and file servers
- a conducive working atmosphere – ceiling height will be an important consideration here
- good storage facilities to accommodate the different types of materials
- an office for the centre manager and staff, and administrative space for the effective organisation and management of the centre.

Excellent resources

- the provision of a comprehensive collection of resources to support the curriculum, matched to the academic needs and abilities of all the pupils, literacy and reading extension, students' personal development and leisure reading
- a generous supply of modern ICT hardware
- information on the resources held throughout the school
- details of resources available from outside the school together with details of special collections.

Opportunities to develop student skills

It is important to:
- continue to develop pupils' literacy skills and encourage their interest in wider reading
- provide support for the development of information handling and learning skills
- develop ICT skills for retrieving and handling information.

A Clear and Effective Set of Policies

Essentially a whole-school approach is needed for the planning, financing, organising and evaluating of the services of the library resource centre, although in some schools this may not be possible. An LRC policy is not so much one policy but a raft of policies which will enable the school to make full use of the centre, set standards and plan for future development. It may well include:

1. A clearly defined budget plan, which takes into account the need to maintain and develop the resource collection, the running costs of the ICT equipment and systems, and includes financial monitoring procedures.

2. Curriculum development information, with details of:
   - the induction programme
   - the school's integrated information skills programme and its method of assessment.

3. A framework for the LRC's involvement in major units of work for each department, to include LRC department liaison, and teaching and learning objectives.

4. Details about staff training, their planned development needs and opportunities.

5. Details about the use of space and priorities for use, before, during and after the school day.

6. A whole-school resource selection policy.

7. The policy for editing and deleting resources, books, ICT, and so on.

8. The LRC's role in supporting and promoting the school's behaviour management policies and practices.

9. The role of the librarian or resource centre manager in the school and the lines of responsibility to the senior management team.

10. The support available from outside agencies, such as the school library service, the public library, the museum service and the careers service.

11. The LRC's policy on Internet filtering, supervision of use, and access.

The LRC policy will be closely related to the LRC development plan – both policy and plan are interlinked. (See *Policy Making and Development Planning for the Secondary School Library*, SLA Guideline, forthcoming Summer 2002.)

The size of the library resource centre team will depend on the size of the school and budgeting constraints. The team will carry out the day-to-day management of the LRC within the policy framework and support the development of curriculum-related skills. A full team may consist of:

1. A librarian or resource centre manager

2. Resource assistants to provide support for the day-to-day management

3. Technical assistants, to provide particularly ICT assistance for problems with computer equipment

4. Classroom assistants to help with homework/learning activities at break-times and lunch-times, and with after-school clubs.

When the centre is working effectively with its services at full stretch, there will be need for increased staffing. They, in turn, will require more space at the counter and in the office – for supporting pupils and for general administration. It is always sensible to plan for expansion at the initial planning stage of a building or refurbishment programme.

Partnerships

Schools are now investigating and setting up partnerships with other service providers in order to maximise the use of resources, equipment and expertise.

Computer suites, set up in partnership with community education providers or similar services, as part of the LRC or adjacent to the centre, are particularly valuable as they can be open beyond the school day. These possibilities should be thoroughly investigated, again at the planning stage, as accommodation and equipment requirements may change in the light of these partnerships, and extra funding and sponsorship may be available through external agencies to meet capital costs or to develop some of the services.

Accommodation

Carefully thought out and thoroughly discussed planning of the library resource centre accommodation is vital. This should be carried out by a focus group of the school's library staff, teachers, resource assistants and ICT specialists, chaired perhaps by a member of the school's senior management team, working with a representative from the school library service, others from the senior management team, architects and LEA officials. Site aspect, overall planning requirements and consents, access points and health and safety requirements, including fire exits, will need to be considered at this early planning stage.

It will be useful to visit as wide a range of LRCs as possible before embarking on the school's own design, and take your line manager and/or head teacher with you. Make sure you consider at this early stage the possible arrangement and amount of shelving you will need. Consider also study (quiet) areas, ICT provision, special units, fittings and furniture. Expertise and experience in library design is available through school library services, and their staff will be pleased to advise on visits to other school libraries. Companies specialising in the sale of library furniture and fittings also offer a free advisory and design service (see page 23).

The site

The LRC should have a central location with an entrance that is as accessible as possible to all staff and students, including the disabled, and to all departments. Remember, too, the library's aspect. If it is north facing it may be rather dark, but if it is south facing will it receive too much bright light? It should not be a route between teaching areas, and ideally it should be situated on the ground floor.

When considering a new site, all areas of the school should be examined. It may be possible to exchange the present site for a more central location, or to knock through into an adjacent room to create additional space. An open area is far more flexible than a number of small rooms. If walls cannot be removed between adjoining rooms, it may be possible to create arches. These would give some privacy and divide areas while still allowing good supervision of the centre.

Flexible use of space can be further achieved if the LRC is close to the ICT suite, the lecture theatre, and other quiet study areas.

Access

Clear signs to the centre will be needed in prominent places throughout the school.

Care must be taken in planning access for pupils and teachers with disabilities. There should be wheelchair access to all parts of the centre and turning circles for wheelchairs should be considered at the early stages of planning the layout.

Size

The size of the school LRC will relate to the school's overall accommodation. The School Library Association recommends that the resource centre should be able to accommodate comfortably 10 per cent of the school's population at one time for study and private reading. This figure will increase if the sixth form is a large proportion of the total school population (in 14 to 18 age range schools or sixth-form colleges). Additional library space in other parts of the school should be considered as part of the total LRC accommodation – perhaps the school has a separate junior or sixth-form library space.

It is therefore recommended that generally a formula of 10 per cent of the minimum teaching area be applied. This is the minimum space in which it is possible to carry out effectively the functions of the school's library and information service.

Main areas

The ideal LRC should consist of:

- fiction loan area: books and audio-visual storage
- non-fiction loan area: books and audio-visual storage
- an ICT area for Internet and CD-ROM use and catalogue access
- video viewing and conferencing area
- reference or small quick reference section
- audio-visual materials
- newspapers/periodicals section
- maps/charts collections
- careers collection
- study spaces
- informal seating/browsing area
- display areas
- counter area
- librarian's office/workroom
- equipment storage
- library sales display area
- security system
- secure bag and coat area near to the entrance
- sixth-form quiet study area (if required)

Atmosphere

Whether the intention is to plan a large, new, purpose-built LRC or to renovate and refurbish an existing one, the creation of the right atmosphere is essential. The LRC should be welcoming, efficiently organised, exciting and should include:

- soft furnishings
- plants
- displays
- ceramics

- paintings
- other decorative features.

A colour scheme should be decided on from the beginning, and remember not to choose items which clash with the chosen scheme. An attractive and durable carpet is essential for the whole area and should extend under all bookcases and units so that they can be rearranged in the future. Carpet tiles are preferable as these can be changed in areas of high use. A heavy duty barrier carpet directly inside the door will help to preserve the main carpet.

Natural light is an important factor in the library, but take care to balance the amount of window space with the need to use wall space for bookshelves. A library with many large windows will feel very light, but this will mean having to position a large number of shelving units in the centre. Placing as much shelving as possible on the walls allows the central space to be used for browsing and study areas, and is more likely to give an uncluttered feel to the whole library.

It is essential that there is sufficient heating and ventilation, and adequate lighting throughout the LRC, particularly in the display and study areas. Nothing is worse for studying than a room that is too hot, too cold or too stuffy. However, light shining directly on to computer screens will make them difficult to read. Books and spine labels will fade over time in areas of bright sunlight and cheaper paperback fiction will quickly deteriorate.

Shelving and furnishings

It is worth choosing the best shelving and furnishings that the school can afford, even if this means purchasing items over a number of years. The majority of the books and a range of non-book items can be shelved together in one sequence on wall and island shelving units. The arrangement of fiction and non-fiction should be planned in logical sequences with, if possible, enough flexibility to allow for display within those sequences. The plan should allow for as much flexibility as possible.

It is important to consider access and use when planning the layout and organisation of shelving and storage units. Who will want to use which resources and when? Seating and study areas, for example, should not block access to heavily used areas of shelving. This will cause nuisance and disturbance all round.

The wall shelving, computer benching and counter all need to be fixed, while the other units can be moved as the LRC develops. Some shelving systems create impenetrable barriers to vision and light. A system which is more open will provide an airier feel and better sight lines for support and supervision. Users are therefore likely to feel more relaxed and make more focused use of the resources.

Amateur or custom-built shelving units are hardly ever successful and usually need to be replaced within a few years. The system should be flexible and adjustable, with interchangeable shelves and fittings for different types of media. The School Library Association recommends that the maximum height for wall shelving units should be 1800mm, and 1500mm for island units; with the length of individual shelves between 750 and 1000mm and the depth 175 to 250mm. Deciding on a standard length and depth for shelves will make them much more interchangeable. Deeper shelving is available but will usually be required only for some careers material and for larger reference books.

A flexible library shelving system is made up of standard components which enable the shelving to be tailored to the individual library and allow for change and growth in the future. Low island units should be placed on castors or heavy duty mobile bases for easy movement, but not so easy that unsupervised students can move them around!

The two main types of shelving are wooden and metal, and metal shelving is available in a number of attractive colours. End panels for shelving are available in wood, metal and fabric-covered pinboard, and the choice made here will affect the overall atmosphere of the library. Guiding should be provided for all main sections, bays, tiers and shelves.

Variety of shelving units

The following fittings are available for shelving units:

- audio and video cassette and CD shelves
- corner shelves for linking shelving bays
- browser boxes
- desk plates
- display shelves, boards and panels
- divided shelves
- inclined shelves suitable for paperbacks
- leaflet/brochure shelves
- lifting display and storage units
- magazine display and storage shelves
- media display trays
- paperback shelves
- retractable reference shelves
- tiered multi-purpose display shelves
- bay end guiding
- guiding fixtures
- depressible title strips for canopies and shelves
- book supports – suspended and back edge
- canopies
- end panels with display fittings or leaflet racks

Rolling stack systems are available if storage of large quantities of material, not on open access, is required. These units allow for a greater density of storage and are particularly suitable for ground-floor office and storeroom use. They sometimes require strengthened floors and are often hugely expensive. Few are used in school LRCs.

Media storage units

Special storage will be needed for the following non-book items:

- periodicals – display and storage
- study folders/information files
- wall charts/maps/posters
- CD-ROMs, videos and computer software.

With some systems there is a full range of matching accessories including display boards, magazine racks, mobile display cases, drawers, cupboards, pigeon holes and stationery storage facilities.

Seating areas

As stated previously, the School Library Association recommends that the library should be able to seat at least 10 per cent of the school's population at any one time. In a library of 250 square metres and upwards, with careful planning it is possible to provide seating for two classes as well as for small groups, individual study, and computer workstations. The two main seating areas need to be separated, perhaps with shelving units or free-standing display/divider screens, to give some privacy to teachers working with larger groups. The counter, reprographics, and listening and viewing areas will create noise, so these should not normally be positioned too close to quiet study areas, but the counter should be close enough to allow for supervision.

Class groups, small groups and individuals will all need study tables and chairs. Tables for four to six people are best: larger tables are cumbersome and lead to an inflexible arrangement of furniture. Informal chairs and coffee tables should be provided for browsing. All chairs should be chosen to co-ordinate with the colour scheme of the library. Height adjustable tables and workstations are available and are ideally suited for pupils in wheelchairs.

Within these main areas, sufficient power and data points will be needed for using equipment, including televisions and computers.

ICT areas

The role of ICT in the learning resource centre continues to grow in importance and room for future expansion must be considered at the early planning stage. Key questions might be: what sort of LRC do we need now, and what are we likely to need in ten years time?

Indeed, what space for future ICT developments might we need in five years time? DfES architects recommend an additional 10 per cent of floor space to accommodate ICT workstations, and this figure may well increase. When developing a new resource centre it is essential to consider installing a library network. Consequently, it is vital that the siting of the workstations and networked printers is included early in the planning process so that adequate cabling can be installed. Cabling for a network, or for stand-alone machines, should be neat and unobtrusive and, above all, safe.

The computers should be located close to the counter where it should be easier for staff both to monitor their use and provide assistance to students. Computer workstations can be sited in groups along the walls or on island banks. It is essential to consider the number of computers in each group carefully, to allow effective support for small groups of students in the use of the Internet and software applications, and to discourage large amounts of noise and movement. The use of the LRC as a computer room should be discouraged.

The School Library Association recommends that benching of at least 800mm in depth should be used or that purpose-designed units with cable carriers are purchased. Work surfaces should be non-reflective. Make sure that adequate working space is allowed beside the computers, as well as space for peripherals such as printers, scanners and CD-ROM drives. Although anti-glare screens can be fitted, the positioning of monitors needs careful consideration as glare from lighting in the library or from windows may create problems for users. The provision of a large screen for at least one terminal will help when demonstrating how to search the Internet and will also benefit partially–sighted pupils. It would also be advisable to buy an LRC electronic whiteboard for use when making group and class presentations.

Computer chairs will be required for each workstation. These should be of the five castor based variety, height adjustable using gas lift, and have adjustable backs and seat rakes.

A wide range of individual and modular computer workstations are available including:

- corner cluster units
- height adjustable computer centres with up to six stations

- computer tables for stand-alone machines or mix and match shapes and sizes
- units with four work surfaces, sliding keyboard shelf, a middle shelf and two fixed shelves
- interlinking units to create suites of continuous benching
- kidney-shaped computer desks
- computer study carrels for three, four, six or eight people. These include desk screens to separate workstations and reduce noise levels
- height adjustable cantilever design units which are ideal for people using wheelchairs
- circular formations of workstations of varying sizes.

It is important to check the stability of each unit and that adequate cable carriers are incorporated.

Counter

The counter is the hub of the LRC and provides control, supervision and information for the whole area. Whatever its height, the counter should not form a barrier to users, and a dual-height counter should ensure equal access for all users, particularly students and teaching staff in wheelchairs. It is important that the counter area is well planned and large enough to accommodate a computerised issue system and printer, a telephone, and adequate workspace. Lockable drawers will be needed for stationery items.

There are various options here: a custom-built counter; a system available through library suppliers in modular form; or a large office desk. Chairs with castors are best for this area. It is always useful to provide a bay of shelving behind the counter, and don't forget space for several trolleys.

The counter should be close to the main entrance and preferably adjacent to the office and workroom. This will be a busy thoroughfare, so adequate circulation space for pupils is essential around the counter. Remember too that if security gates are used, they must be placed at a specified distance from computers. If a security system is to be installed, this will have a bearing upon the position of the counter, so it is essential here to ask the advice of the system's supplier.

If a self-issue terminal is to be provided, this should be close to the main counter.

Catalogue

It is important that students and staff have adequate access to the computerised library catalogue. This can be achieved by the use of stand-alone machines but preferably through a network. This network may be exclusive to the LRC or may extend beyond, and be available to staff and students in other parts of the school. A printer must be available to enable the results of searches to be printed by staff and students. If a card catalogue is used, this should be adjacent to the counter.

Photocopier

A photocopier is an essential tool in the library and should be placed adjacent to the counter to allow for supervision and easy payment for copies.

Display

To encourage greater use of the resource centre, a shop type display window can usefully be included in the plan. A lockable display unit in another part of the school can also be used to publicise the library to a wider audience. Within the centre, every opportunity should be taken to display materials and teaching and learning ideas effectively. The displays should be varied and changed frequently. Display shelves, units and fabric-covered display boards will be required, and lighting will enhance these areas.

Careers library

The careers library may be located in or adjacent to the main library. Space will be required for the full range of materials. A computer will be needed to run careers packages, and additional hardware such as a printer or CD-ROM drive will be needed. A display area, space for private study, and a browsing area should also be made available. The careers officer/careers co-ordinator will most likely need interview space, within the library or adjacent to it.

Administration area

Adequate space is essential for the efficient administration of the LRC and, perhaps, for the preparation of teaching and learning materials. Don't be fobbed off with vague promises – make sure you do get enough admin space! The following need to be accommodated:

1. **Office/workroom** This area should be not less than 20 square metres and adjacent to the counter. Windows between the office/workroom and the public area are a good idea. They will help to give an unrestricted view and enable staff working behind the scenes to supervise the centre. Shelving is required for materials on closed access, such as computer software and video cassettes. Workbenches with drawers are preferable to desks as they are more versatile. The following items will also be required:
   - issue and display equipment
   - computer workstations for cataloguing new acquisitions
   - filing cabinets
   - book trolleys
   - storage crates
   - perhaps telephone point and ICT connections.

2. **Equipment and storage** This area will need plenty of power points, large rack type shelving, adequate work surfaces, and perhaps an area for off-air recording. The floor space should be non-slip, uncluttered and free from all obstacles. Adequate provision will need to be made for ventilation, and particular care should be taken over the health and safety aspects of the room.

3. **Design and production of materials** If your working area is also part of the school's main reprographic centre, a minimum area of between 14 and 16 square metres is recommended. This is over and above the recommended area for the LRC. It should include wall and island shelving for storage of materials, and heavy-duty work surfaces for machinery. Generous storage space for raw materials is desirable and a convenient water supply essential. If a darkroom is planned, LEA advice must be sought because of the need to conform to regulations concerning water supply, waste disposal and safety.

The following is a basic checklist for equipment in a library resource centre:

- ICT equipment – computers with relevant software for word-processing and spreadsheets, etc, speakers and headphones
- CD-ROMs and DVDs
- Internet/e-mail facilities
- digital camera
- scanner
- laptop computers
- LCD multimedia projector
- video recorders/interactive equipment
- televisions/monitors
- overhead projectors
- projection screens
- audio-visual equipment trolleys
- radio/cassette players
- double radio/cassette recorder
- recording time switches
- cassette players and headphones
- headphones
- flip chart and stand
- whiteboard
- electronic whiteboard
- photocopier
- electric stapler
- collator
- spiral binding (or similar binding) equipment
- lettering machines
- paper trimmer
- music centre of some sort to play background music as required

A Refurbishment Project

The success of the learning resource centre depends on the atmosphere created by the colour scheme, design and layout, as well as the materials, information sources and staffing available.

Where the space and location of the centre are satisfactory, schools may well need to plan a refurbishment programme. After all, with heavy and constant use a library may well soon begin to look tired. Any library make-over/ refurbishment should meet all the criteria established for new buildings. Schools refurbishing their LRC on a limited budget should plan and prioritise expenditure, which may have to be planned over a number of years.

Although some improvements may be effected by rearranging existing furniture and equipment, the greatest impact in terms of appearance and use of resources will be achieved by providing appropriate modern shelving. New furnishings and carpets will further enhance the centre, as will a new coat of paint.

Opposite is a list of common problems found in school LRCs, with suggested solutions!

Problem	Possible Solution
Location Library resource centre isolated and away from the centre of the school and main teaching areas	Consider a central site, exchange present accommodation for a more appropriate ground floor location
Size Below minimum size for the school population	Extend accommodation into adjoining rooms or relocate, or consider an extension
Atmosphere Unwelcoming, cluttered, oppressive	Use an attractive colour scheme for all furnishings and décor. Discard unnecessary and damaged furniture, units and equipment. Choose a shelving system offering fittings for multimedia resources
Layout Unimaginative and inappropriate use of space	Plan the layout to reflect the various patterns of use, including ▪ location of seating areas ▪ arrangement of resources in coherent sequences ▪ need for circulation space ▪ need for supervision ▪ use of computers and other equipment ▪ variations in noise levels
Shelving Inflexible unattractive shelving	Provide a flexible and adjustable shelving system, giving storage for a wide range of resources
Counter High counter unit forming a barrier	Provide a lower counter which is more suitable for those using computers or for enquiry work
Flooring Worn carpet or uneven floor covering	Provide an attractive, durable carpet or carpet tiles to reflect the décor of the centre and absorb noise
Chairs Dated and worn	Purchase new chairs or re-upholster to achieve a co-ordinated image

Problem	Possible Solution
Lighting Inadequate lighting, preventing rearrangement of shelving and study areas	Improve lighting levels throughout the LRC, especially in study and display areas
Windows Unsuitable and worn curtains. Glare from sun on computer screens	Remove curtains and replace with blinds. Fit anti-glare film to windows
Display Lack of display space within the LRC, and facilities to promote the centre elsewhere in the school	Purchase free-standing screens and cover boards with fabric to match the colour scheme. Provide a display window or case (preferably lockable) outside the library
Guiding Worn and inadequate guiding	Buy some purpose-made guiding and signs from one of the specialist library suppliers
ICT Existing equipment unsuitable for the introduction of a computerised library management system, or the networking of CD-ROMS, or easy access to the Internet	Investigate appropriate software and hardware
Lack of compatibility with other school ICT equipment and networks	Investigate including the LRC on the school network/intranet

A well designed and resourced library resource centre is essential to every secondary school, for it has the potential to make a major contribution to teaching and learning. It is important that the school LRC is designed to the highest standards and that the plan is sufficiently flexible to meet the changing patterns of learning in both the short and medium term. Adequate funds need to be made available for quality shelving, furniture and equipment, as well as for resources and, of course, staffing. The future use of the LRC will be greatly influenced by both decisions and investment made at the initial stages of a building or refurbishment programme.

Curriculum changes, recent literacy initiatives, and far-reaching developments in ICT call for sophisticated information handling skills. The LRC, therefore, should be at the forefront of these changes. The learning which takes place in the classroom is enhanced by learning within the library. The literacy, study and information skills acquired, developed and practised there enable the students to become more effective and confident as independent learners.

A well-resourced LRC provides teachers with a new teaching environment, which will help them to meet the challenges and opportunities in education today. All staff and governors should be part of this development to provide students with the resources and skills required for lifelong learning.

Further Reading

British Educational Communications & Technology Agency (BECTa) produce a number of advice sheets on ICT which may be useful.
See their website: <www.becta.org.uk/technology/itadvice.html>

COGHLAN, V., QUIGLEY, P. and WALTON, R. (Editors) *Library File: Making a Success of the School Library*
Library Association of Ireland, 1999.   0 94603 736 1

DEWE, MICHAEL *Planning and Designing Libraries for Children and Young People*
Library Association, 1995.   1 85604 100 X

DEPARTMENT FOR EDUCATION AND EMPLOYMENT *Access for Disabled People to School Buildings.*   Bulletin No. 91
HMSO, 1999.   0 11 271062 X

DEPARTMENT FOR EDUCATION AND EMPLOYMENT *Area Guidelines for Schools.*   Building Bulletin No. 82
HMSO, 1996.   0 11 270921 4

DEPARTMENT FOR EDUCATION AND EMPLOYMENT *Guidelines for Environmental Design in Schools.*   Building Bulletin No. 87
HMSO, 1987.   0 11 271013 1

KINNELL, MARGARET *Managing Library Resources in Schools*
Library Association Publishing, 1994.   1 85604 096 8

LEMAIRE, KATHY *Shelf Life, Shelf Matters: Managing Resources in the School Library.*   SLA Guideline
School Library Association, 2001.   1 903446 04 X

SMITH, M., CHARLTON, L. and SPRINGFORD, P. (Editors) *Learning Resources in Secondary Schools: Guidelines for Good Practice*
Cambridge Education Service, 1988.   1 870724 55 0

SOUTHCOMBE, DIANNE and WINKWORTH, LYNN 'Policy Making and Development Planning for the Secondary School Library'.   SLA Guideline
forthcoming, Summer 2002.   1 903446 12 0

TILKE, ANTHONY (Editor) *Guidelines for Secondary School Libraries*
Library Association Publishing, 1998.   1 85604 278 X

Shelving and furniture

Demco (formerly Don Gresswell)
Grange House
2 Geddings Road
Hoddesdon EN11 0NT
For all sales from both mail order catalogues
Tel: 01992 454500
Fax: 01992 448989
e-mail: direct@gresswell.co.uk

Demco Interiors (formerly LFC)
Phoenix House
54 Denington Road
Wellingborough NN8 2QH
For all product requests (and for measuring up individual libraries)
Tel: 01933 445300
Fax: 01933 442764
e-mail: dispatch@lfc-ltd.co.uk

Exclusive Fitted Furniture
Sturminster Newton
Dorset DT10 1AZ
Tel: 01258 472001
Fax: 01258 473884
e-mail: sales@exclusive-furniture.co.uk

Finnmade Furniture Ltd
Lynton House
6 Newlands Lane
Hitchin SG4 9AY
Tel: 01462 452001
Fax: 01462 452002
e-mail: finnmade.furniture @ntlworld.com

Remploy Furniture Group
Bruce Road
Swansea Industrial Estate
Fforestfach
Swansea SA5 4HY
Tel: 01792 560100
Fax: 01792 560167
e-mail: furniture@remploy.co.uk

Euro-Rack
117 Bann Road
Dublin Industrial Estate
Dublin 11
Tel: 00353 1 8307 789

Security systems

3M Library Systems
Customer Technical Services
Easthampstead Road
Bracknell RG12 1JE
Tel: 01344 866485
Fax: 01344 866495
e-mail: library-uk@mmm.com

Plescon Security Products
Unit 9, Sterling Complex
Sproughton Business Park
Farthing Road
Ipswich IP1 5AP
Tel: 01473 747159
Fax: 01473 747259
e-mail: info@plescon.co.uk

Sensormatic Ltd.
Harefield Grove
Rickmansworth Road
Harefield
Uxbridge UB9 6JY
Tel: 01895 873000
Fax: 01895 873901
e-mail: ukmarket@sensormatic.com

Two Example Layouts for a Library Resource Centre

1

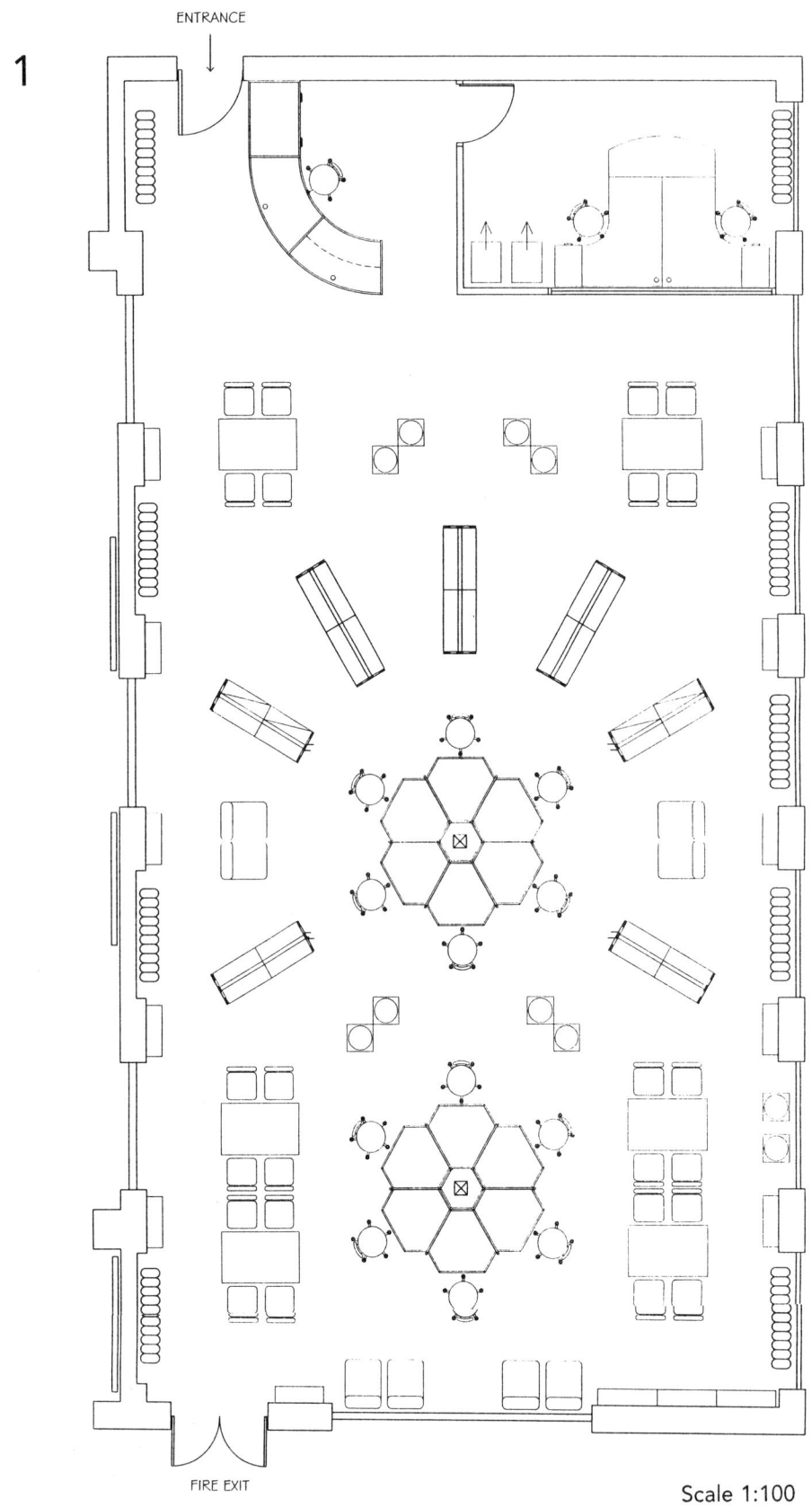

FIRE EXIT

Scale 1:100

For comments on these two layouts, see page 26

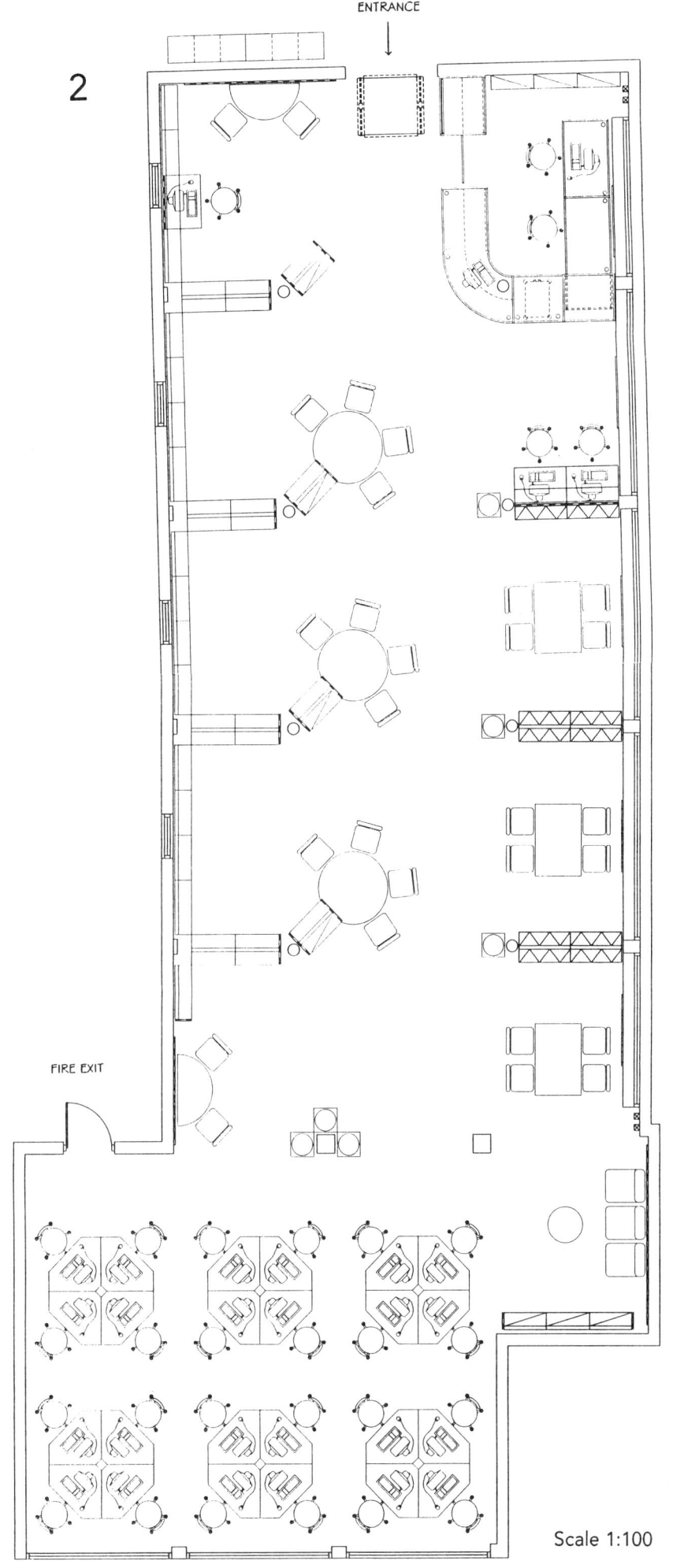

ENTRANCE

2

FIRE EXIT

Scale 1:100

Layout 1

This is very much a library resource centre of the 21st century. Immediately we can see the impact of the integrated ICT and the appealing arrangement of the radially arranged bookshelves. With twelve centrally located computer workstations, seating for twenty-four students at study tables, and a further eight well-spaced comfortable seats for relaxed reading, this is very much a layout for a school that expects to make effective use of its library resource centre to support learning. The seating can cope with a full class and a few more users, and the centre will need more than one member of staff. You will notice that the counter is well positioned by the entrance and that thought has been given to providing staff with some office space. The large office window should provide adequate natural lighting.

Windows on two sides of the LRC help to give an airy feel to the room, and the shelving looks as if it has been arranged to provide good circulation space for users. Staff at the desk and in the office should have a reasonable view of most or all users, thus providing adequate supervision. I am guessing that the fire door, marked on the plan, will be used only in an emergency and not as extra entrance.

The well-spaced bookshelves will need clear bay and shelf guides, and careful thought will need to be given to the sequence of resources.

Layout 2

In the second layout there is a clear divide between the more traditional and the ICT work spaces. With twenty-four ICT workstations in a designated area, and another three near the counter, this LRC is giving clear messages about the importance of ICT in information searching and handling. Twenty-six traditional study spaces, together with some comfortable seating, indicate that this is an LRC that expects to be well used. It will need a minimum of two members of staff to supervise and support pupils during busy times.

Placing the computers together at some distance from the counter area could cause support and supervision problems when the LRC is busy, as could placing the comfortable chairs at the far end of the room. The door opening directly into the ICT area is a fire door. To have had it as a free access point for use of ICT equipment would again have caused supervision problems. Notice the row of lockers for coats and bags near the main entrance.

The shelving is well spaced and interestingly arranged to abut some of the circular study tables. The counter is located by the entrance, which has a security system in place, but in this LRC no space has been allocated for any enclosed, or even partially enclosed, office space. I would guess that space is limited, but when possible library staff do need a secure office area. However, a rather longer and narrower space has been interestingly and creatively used.